Beautiful
The Carole King Musical

Front cover photo by Joan Marcus

ISBN 978-1-4950-8797-4

7777 W. BLUEMOUND RD. P.O. BOX 13819 MILWAUKEE, WI 53213

In Australia Contact:
Hal Leonard Australia Pty. Ltd.
4 Lentara Court
Cheltenham, Victoria, 3192 Australia
Email: ausadmin@halleonard.com.au

Visit Hal Leonard Online at
www.halleonard.com

BEAUTIFUL

Words and Music by
CAROLE KING

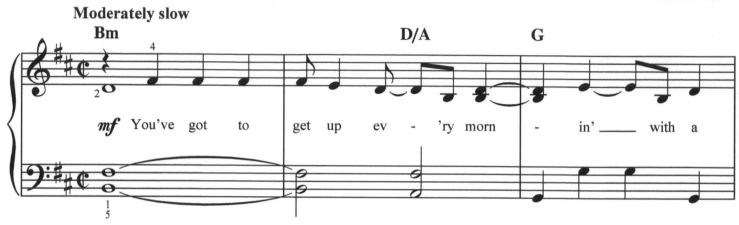

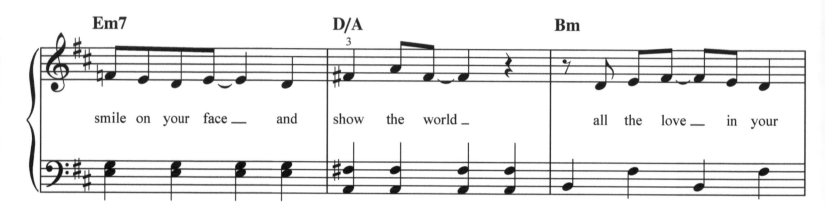

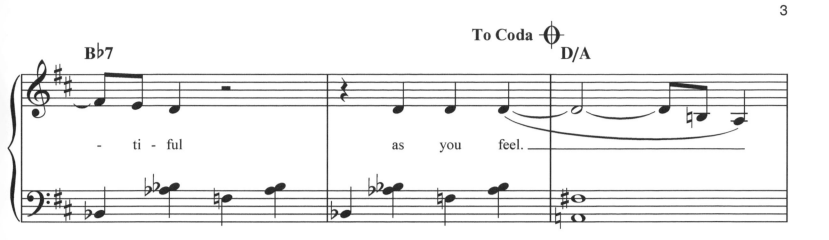

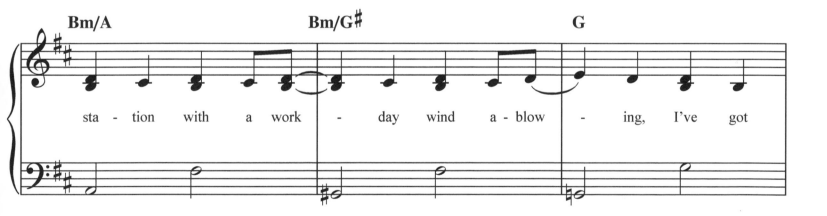

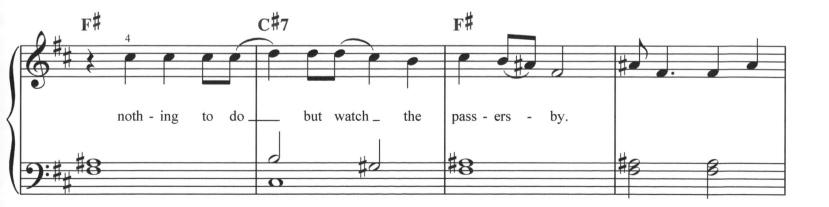

4

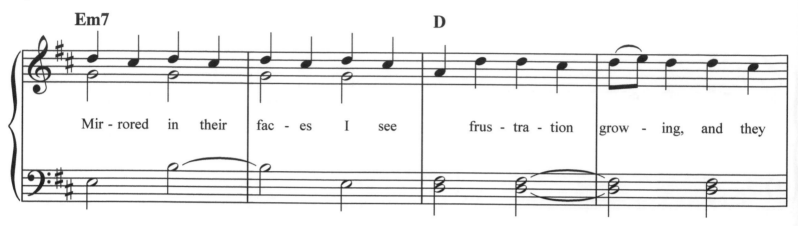

Mir - rored in their fac - es I see frus - tra - tion grow - ing, and they

don't see it show - ing. Why _ do I?

D.C. al Coda

CODA

I have of - ten asked _ my - self the rea - son for the sad -

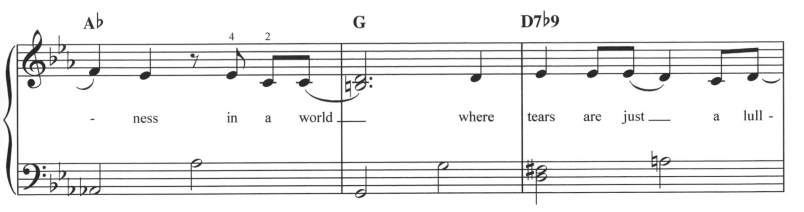

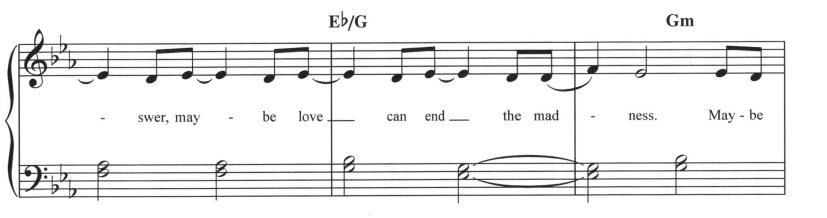

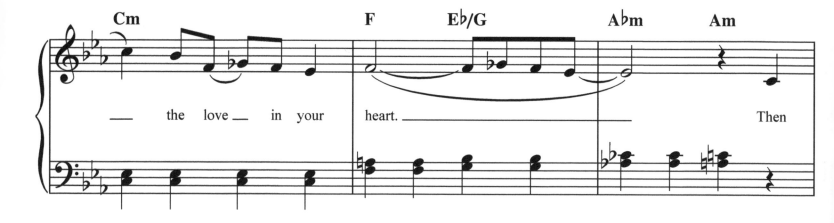

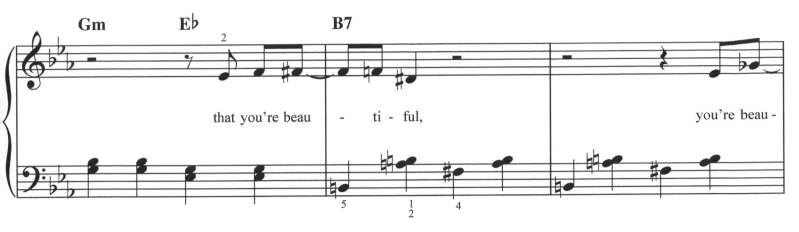

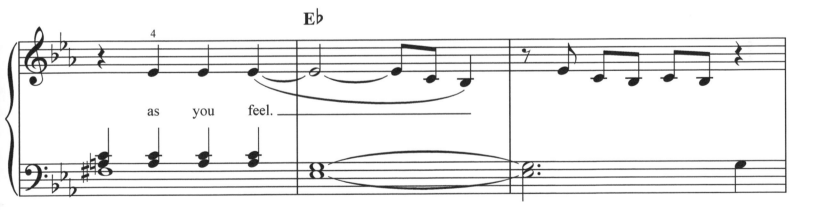

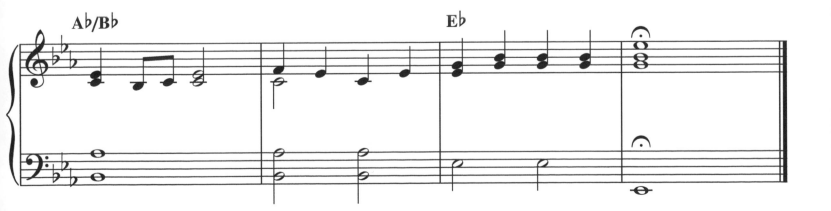

IT'S TOO LATE

Words and Music by CAROLE KING
and TONI STERN

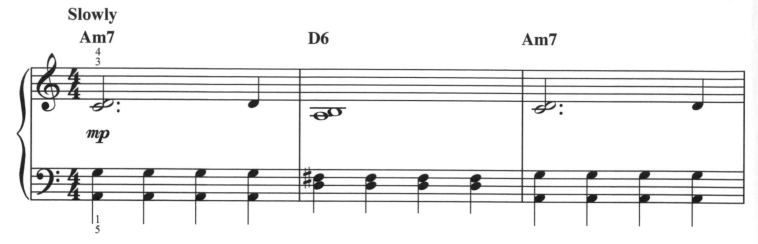

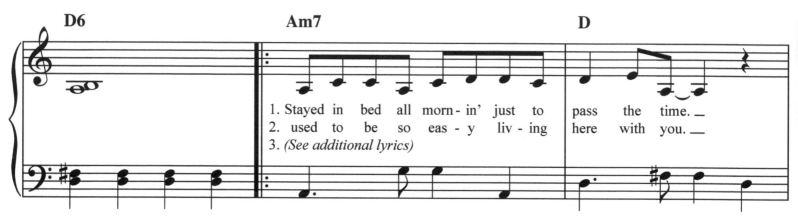

1. Stayed in bed all morn-in' just to pass the time. _
2. used to be so eas-y liv-ing here with you. _
3. *(See additional lyrics)*

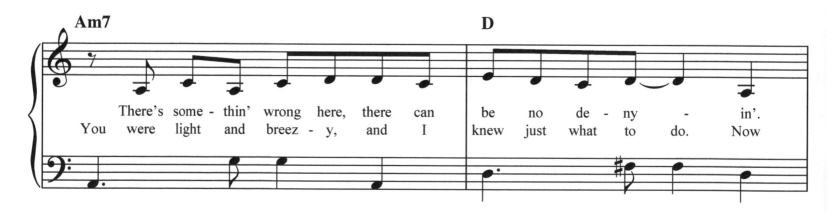

There's some-thin' wrong here, there can be no de-ny - in'.
You were light and breez - y, and I knew just what to do. Now

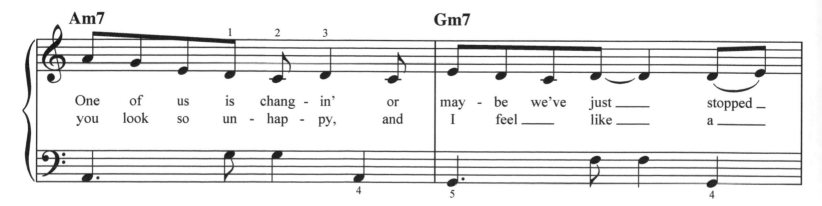

One of us is chang - in' or may-be we've just _____ stopped _
you look so un-hap - py, and I feel _____ like _____ a _____

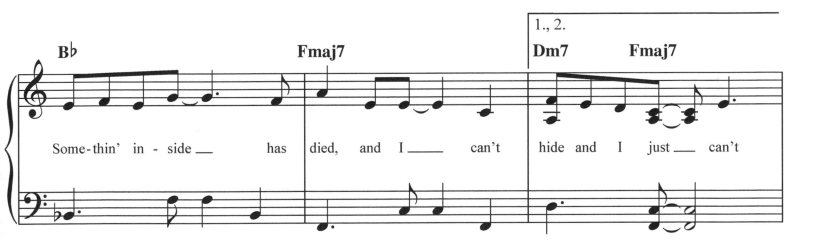

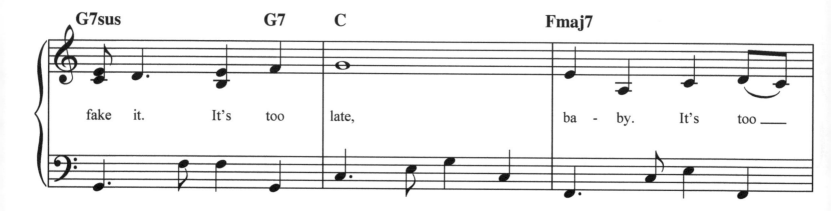

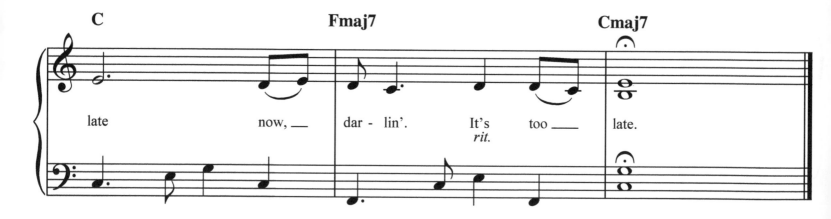

Additional Lyrics

3. There'll be good times again for me and you,
But we just can't stay together.
Don't you feel it, too?
Still I'm glad for what we had
And how I once loved you.
Chorus

I FEEL THE EARTH MOVE

Words and Music by
CAROLE KING

Moderate Rock

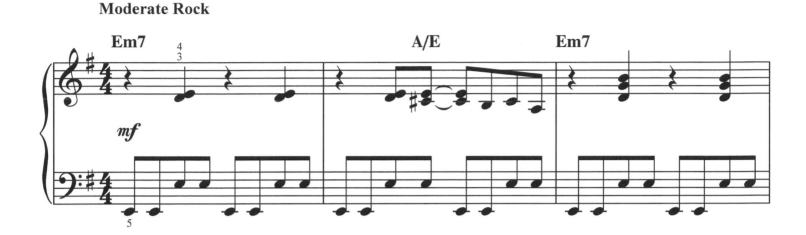

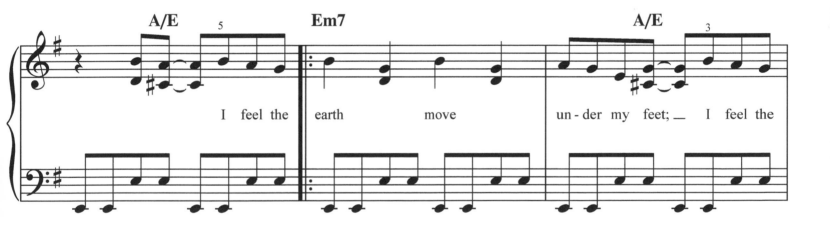

I feel the earth move un-der my feet; __ I feel the

sky __ tum-bl-in' down. __   I feel my heart start to trem-bl-in'

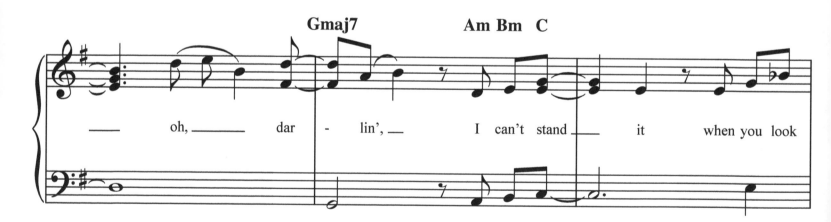

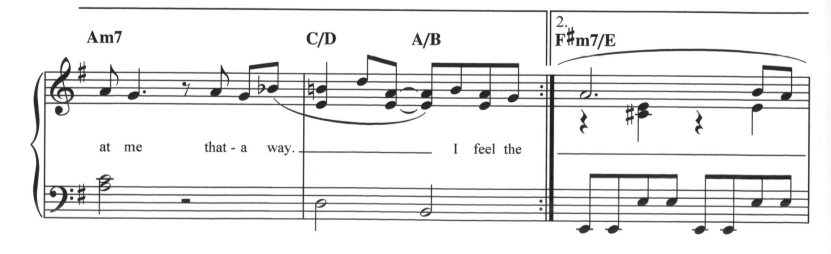

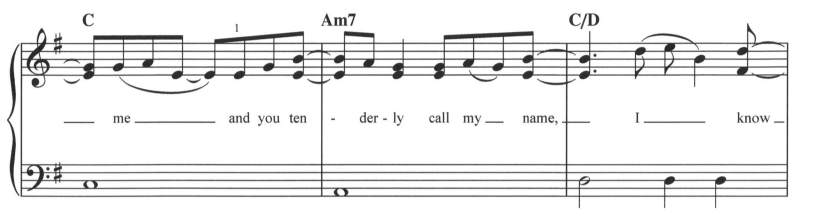

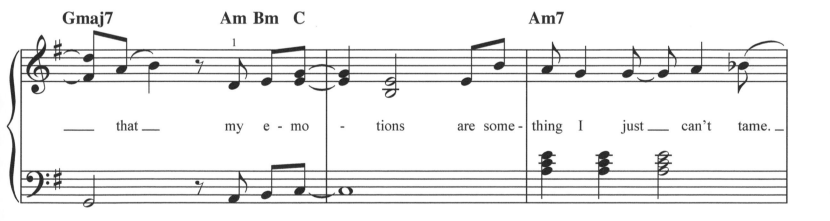

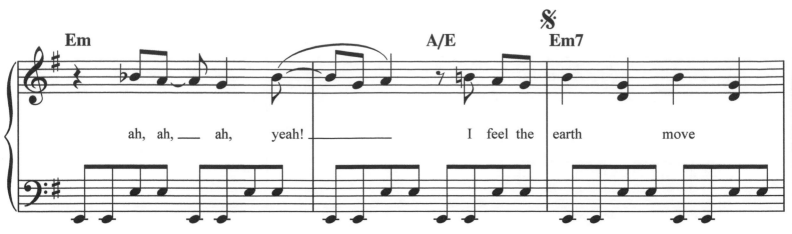

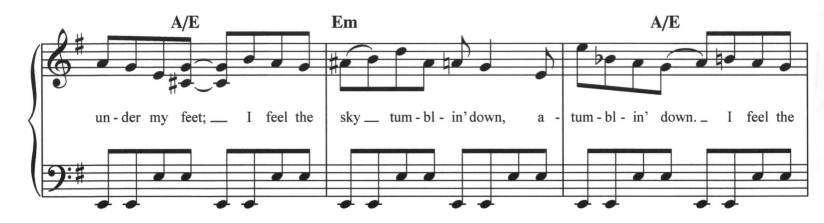

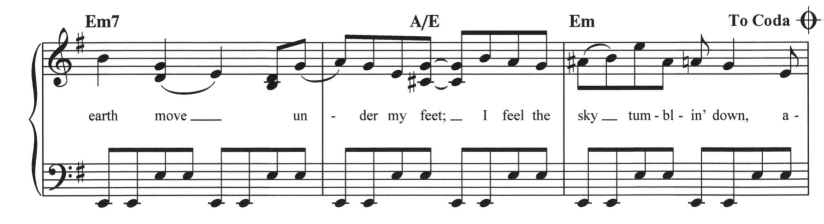

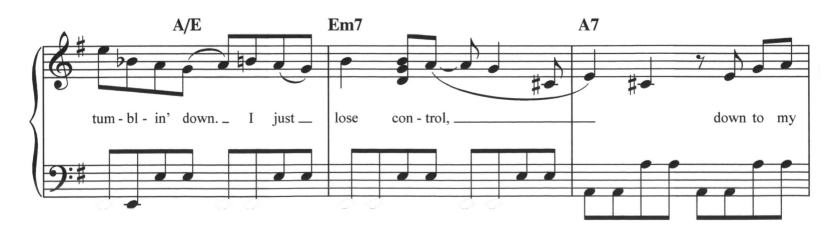

ver - y soul. _____ I get - a hot and cold _____

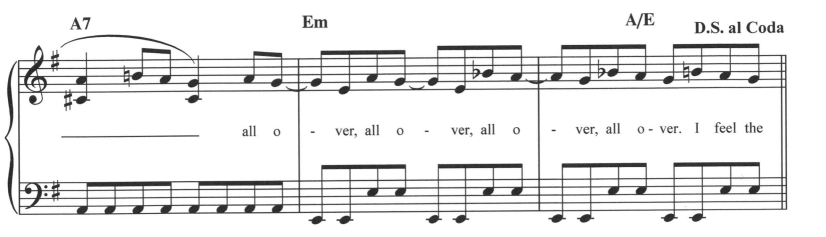

_____ all o - ver, all o - ver, all o - ver, all o - ver. I feel the

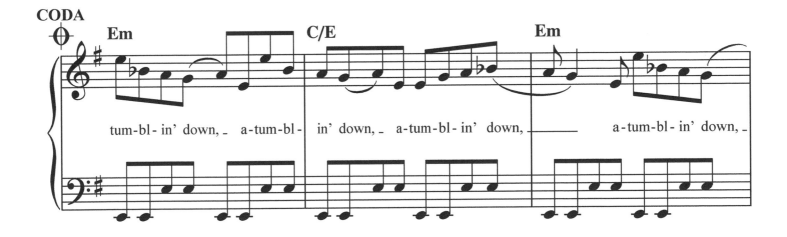

tum-bl-in' down, _ a-tum-bl- in' down, _ a-tum-bl- in' down, _____ a-tum-bl- in' down, _

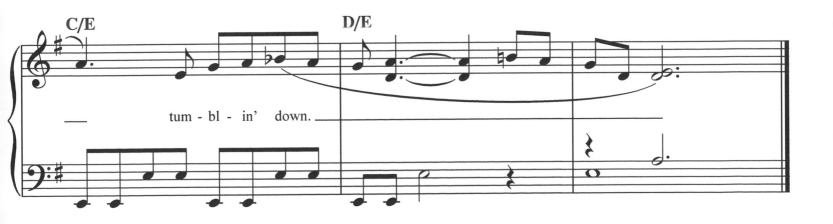

_ tum - bl - in' down. _____

IT MIGHT AS WELL RAIN UNTIL SEPTEMBER

Words and Music by GERRY GOFFIN
and CAROLE KING

What should I write? What can I say? How can I tell you how

much I miss you?

The weath-er
I don't need

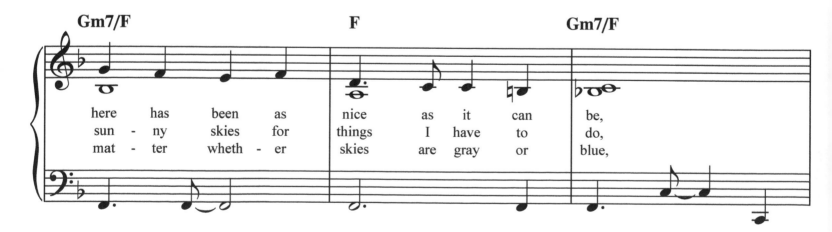

here has been as / nice as it can / be,
sun-ny skies for / things I have to / do,
mat-ter wheth-er / skies are gray or / blue,

al - though it / 'cause I stay / it's rain - ing
does - n't real - ly / home the whole day / in my
mat - ter much to / long and think to / heart 'cause I can't

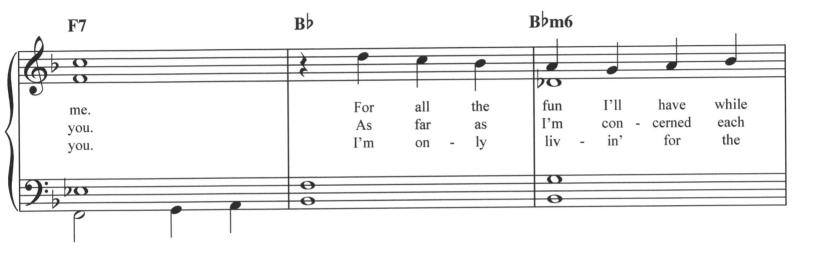

me. / you. / you.

For all the / As far as / I'm on - ly
fun I'll have while / I'm con - cerned each / liv - in' for the

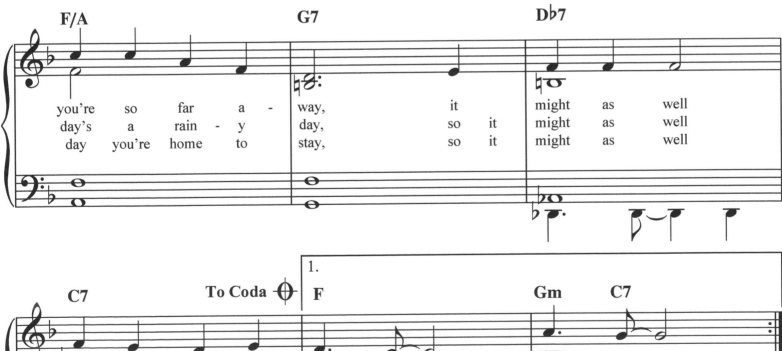

you're so far a - way, / day's a rain - y day, / day you're home to stay,
it / so it / so it
might as well / might as well / might as well

To Coda ⊕

1.

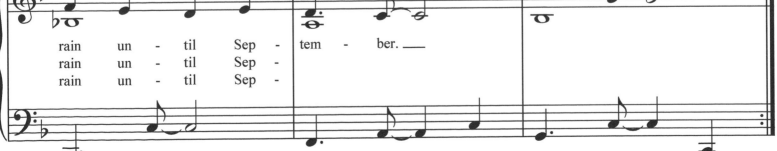

rain un - til Sep - / rain un - til Sep - / rain un - til Sep -
tem - ber.

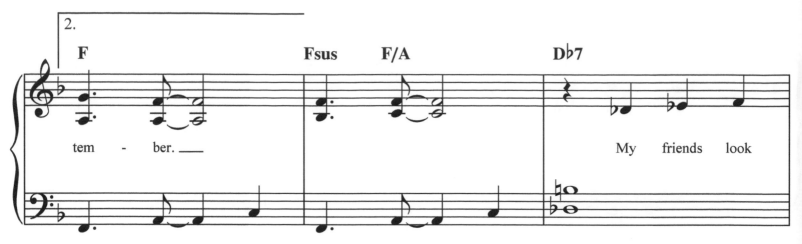

2.

F   Fsus   F/A   Db7

tem - ber. ___   My friends look

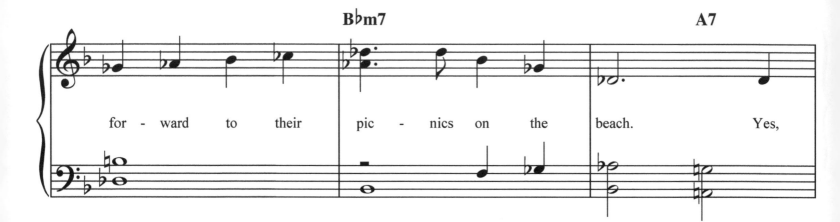

Bbm7   A7

for - ward to their   pic - nics on the   beach.   Yes,

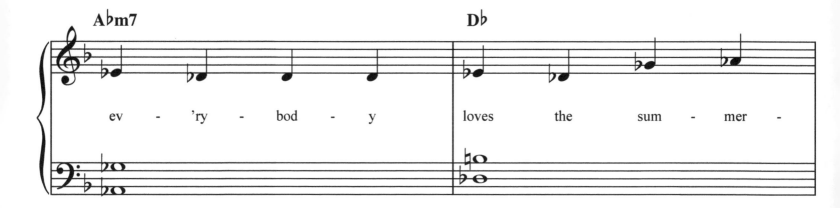

Abm7   Db

ev - 'ry - bod - y   loves the sum - mer -

Gb   3   D7

time. ___   But you know,

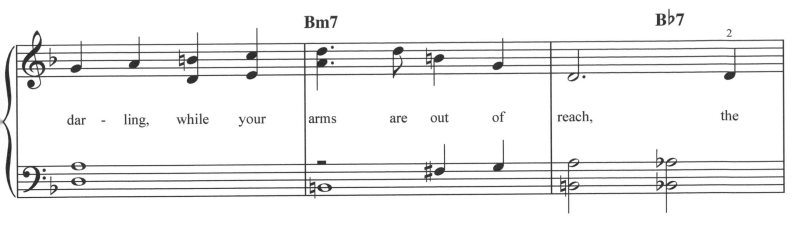

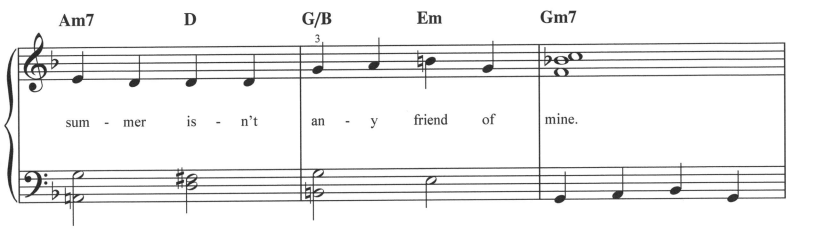

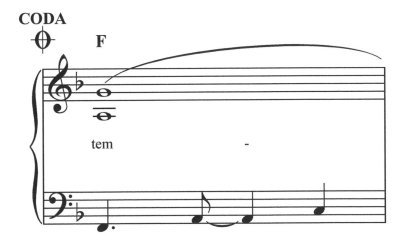

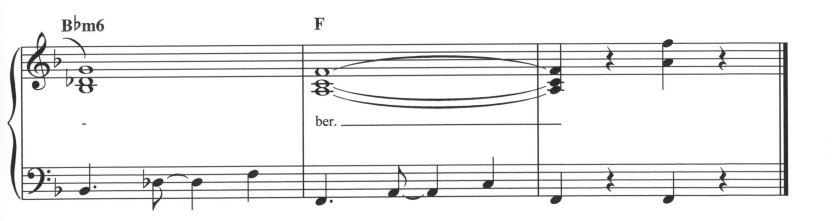

THE LOCO-MOTION

Words and Music by GERRY GOFFIN
and CAROLE KING

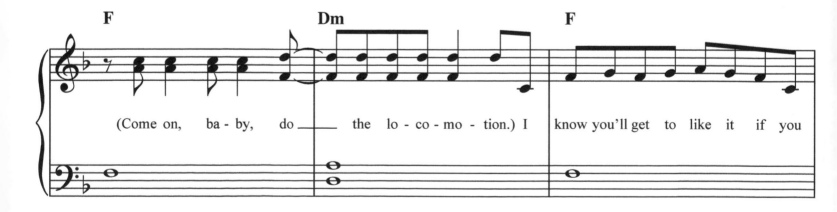

give it a chance __ now. (Come on, ba - by, do __ the lo - co - mo - tion.) My

lit - tle ba - by sis - ter can do it with ease, __ it's eas - i - er than learn - in' your

A - B - C's. __ So come on, come on, do __ the lo - co - mo - tion with

me. You got - ta swing your hips now. Come on,

ba - by, jump up, ____ jump back. ____ Oh, well, I

think you got the knack.

Now that you can do ____ it,
Move a - round the floor ___ in a

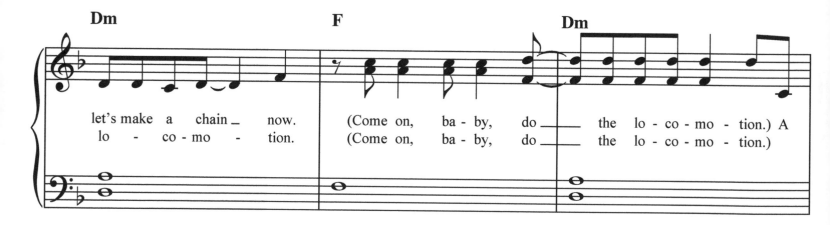

let's make a chain ___ now.
lo - co - mo - tion.

(Come on, ba - by, do ____ the lo - co - mo - tion.) A
(Come on, ba - by, do ____ the lo - co - mo - tion.)

chug - a chug - a mo - tion like a
Do it hold - in' hands _ if ____

rail - road train ___ now.
you get the no - tion.

(Come on, ba - by, do ___
(Come on, ba - by, do ___

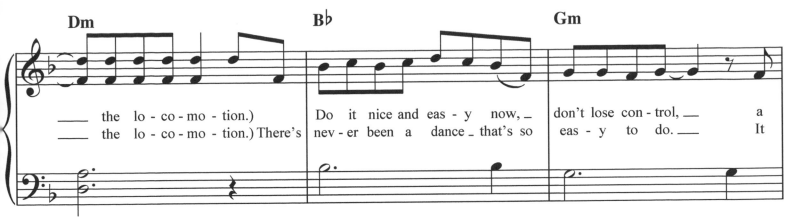

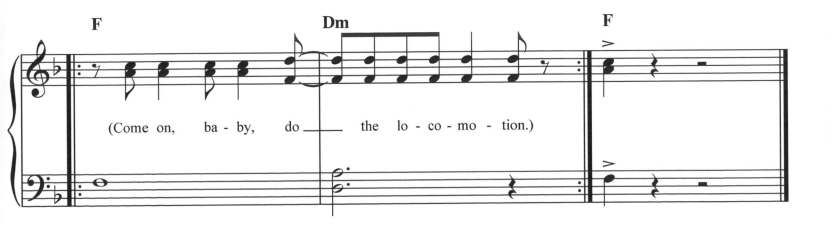

ON BROADWAY

Words and Music by BARRY MANN,
CYNTHIA WEIL, MIKE STOLLER
and JERRY LEIBER

They say the ne - on
They say the wom - en
They say that I won't

lights are bright _ on
treat you fine __ on
last too long __ on

Broad - way; ___
Broad - way, ___
Broad - way. ___

they say there's al - ways
but look - in' at them
I'll catch a Grey - hound

mag - ic in ___ the air.
just gives me ___ the blues.
bus for home, _ they say. _

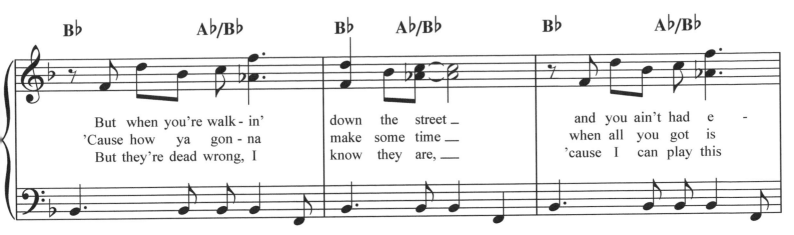

But when you're walk - in'
'Cause how ya gon - na
But they're dead wrong, I

down the street __
make some time __
know they are, __

and you ain't had e -
when all you got is
'cause I can play this

nough to eat, __
one thin dime, __
here gui - tar, __

the glit - ter rubs right
and one thin dime won't
and I won't quit till

1., 2.

off and you're __ no -
e - ven shine __ your

where.
shoes.

3.

I'm a star __ on

Broad - way. __

ONE FINE DAY

Words and Music by GERRY GOFFIN
and CAROLE KING

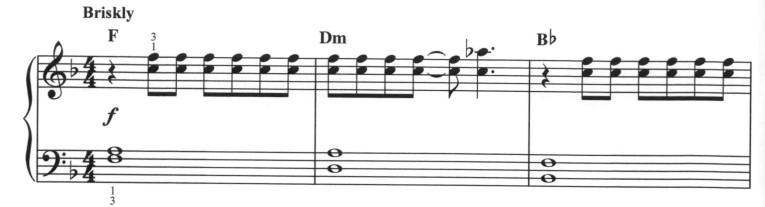

One _____ fine day _____
The arms I long for _____
One _____ fine day _____

you'll look at me, _____ and you will
will o-pen wide, _____ and you'll be
we'll meet once more, _____ and then you'll

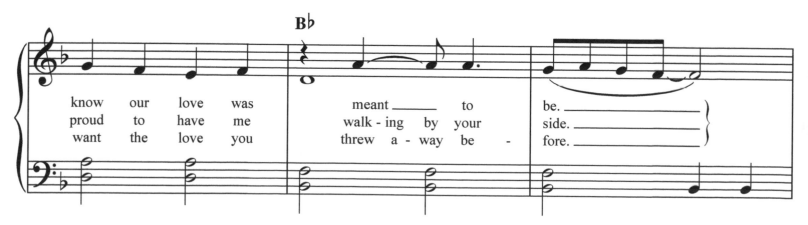

know our love was meant _____ to be. _____
proud to have me walk-ing by your side. _____
want the love you threw a-way be - fore. _____

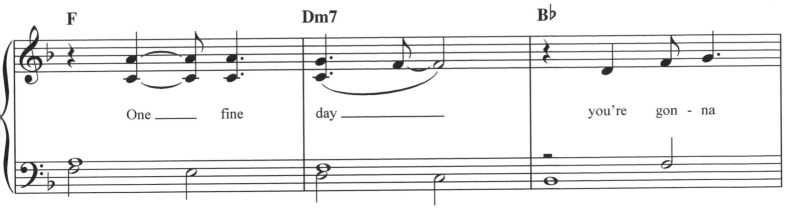

One _____ fine day _____ you're gon - na

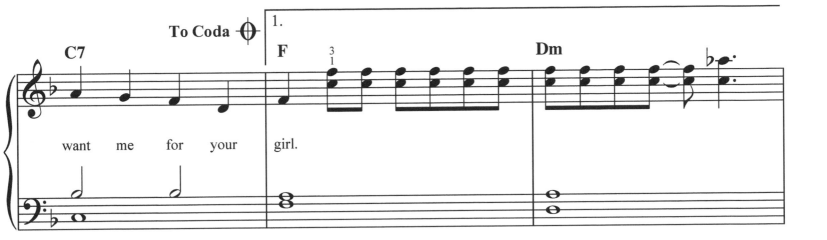

want me for your girl.

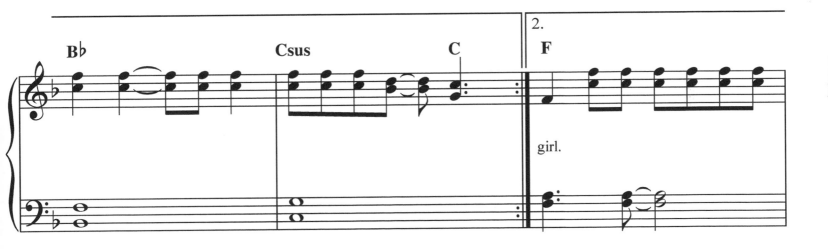

girl.

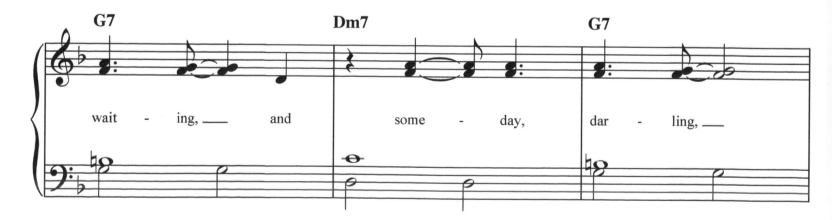

D.S. al Coda

you'll   come   to   me   when you   want   to   set - tle   down,   oh.

CODA

girl.

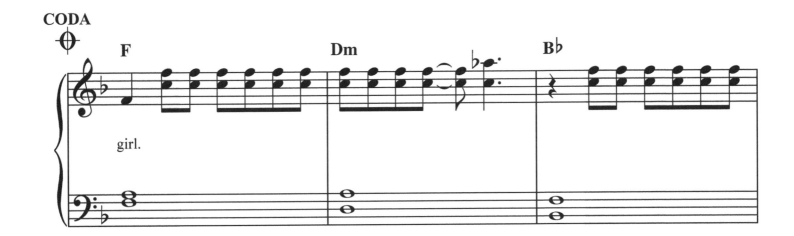

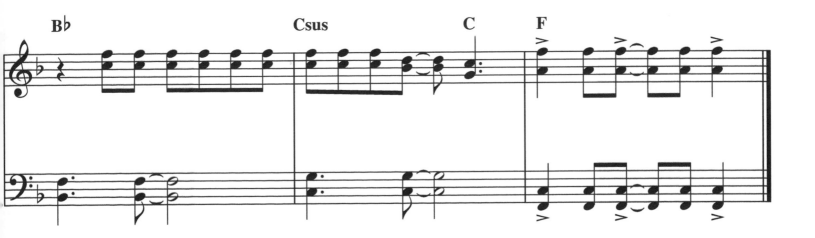

SO FAR AWAY

Words and Music by
CAROLE KING

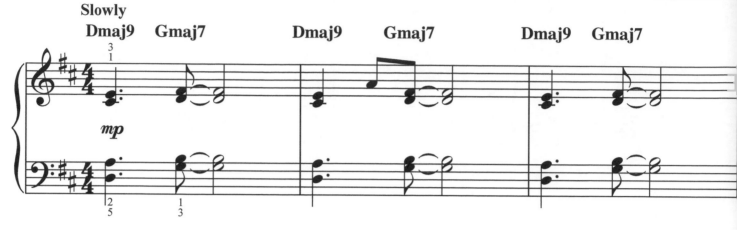

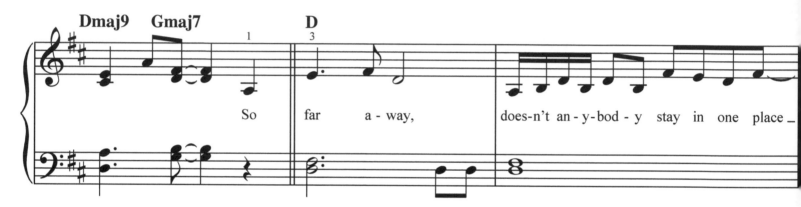

So far a-way, does-n't an-y-bod-y stay in one place

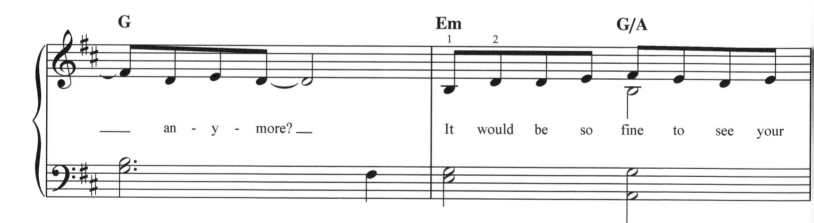

an-y-more?__ It would be so fine to see your

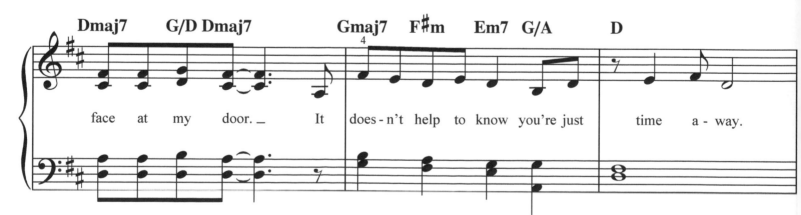

face at my door.__ It does-n't help to know you're just __ time a-way.

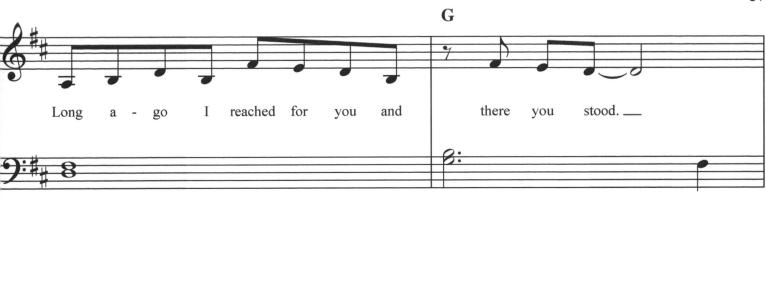

G

Long a-go I reached for you and there you stood. ___

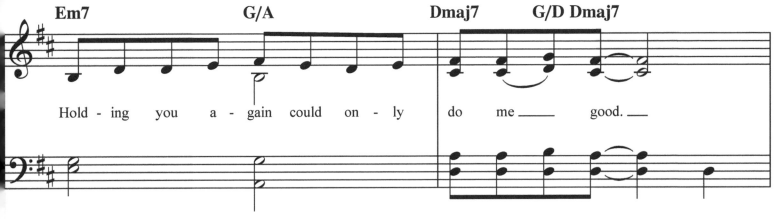

Em7   G/A   Dmaj7   G/D Dmaj7

Hold - ing you a - gain could on - ly do me ___ good. ___

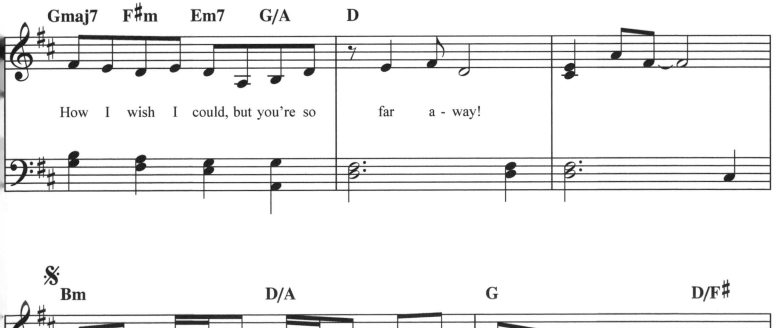

Gmaj7   F#m   Em7   G/A   D

How I wish I could, but you're so far a - way!

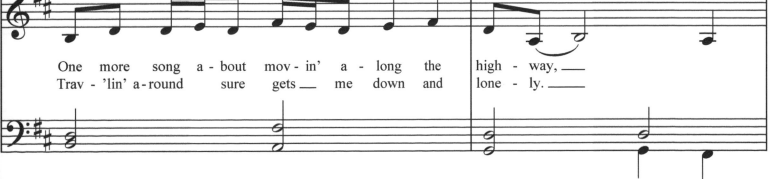

Bm   D/A   G   D/F#

One more song a - bout mov - in' a - long the high - way, ___
Trav - 'lin' a - round sure gets ___ me down and lone - ly. ___

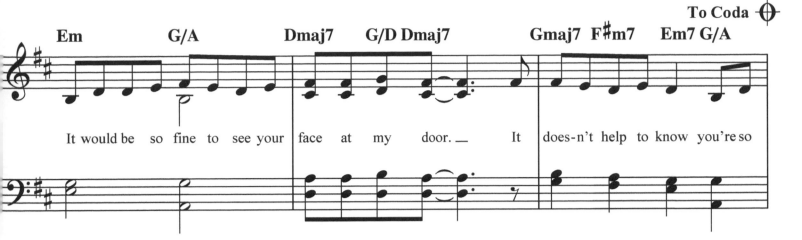

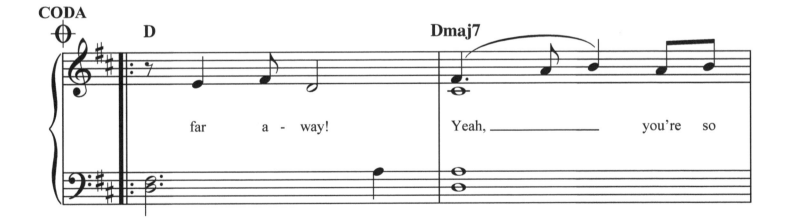

SOME KIND OF WONDERFUL

Words and Music by GERRY GOFFIN
and CAROLE KING

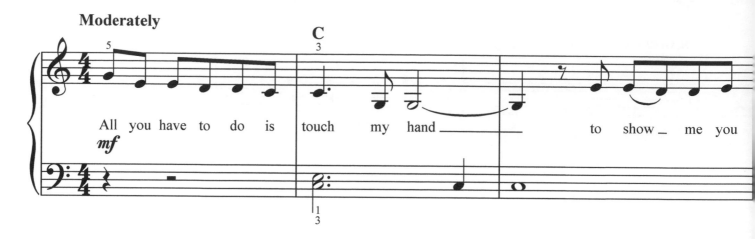

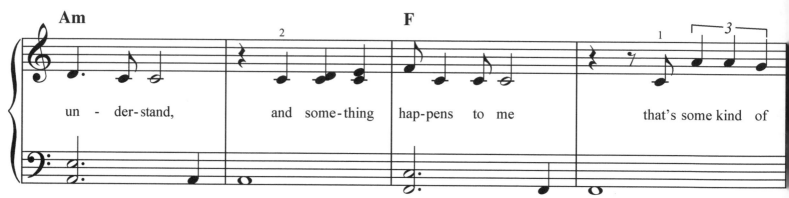

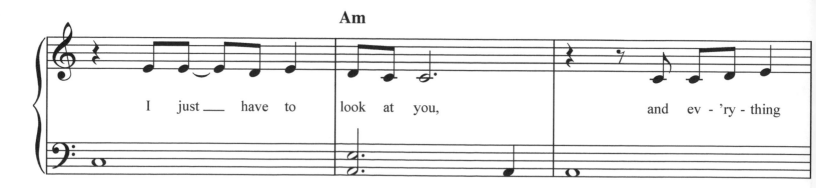

seems to be · · · some kind of won - der - ful!

I know I can't ex - press · · · this feel - ling of

ten - der - ness. There's so · · much I · · want · · to say,

but the right words just don't · come my way. I just know when I'm in

your em - brace ___ this world ___ is a hap - py place,

and some - thing hap - pens to me that's some kind of

won - der - ful! Some kind ___ of won - der - ful!

Some kind of won - der - ful, won - der - ful, won - der - ful, won - der - ful!

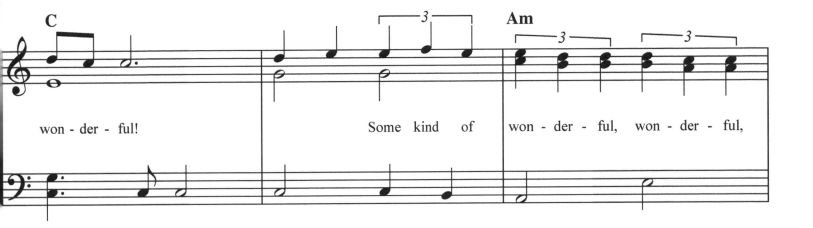

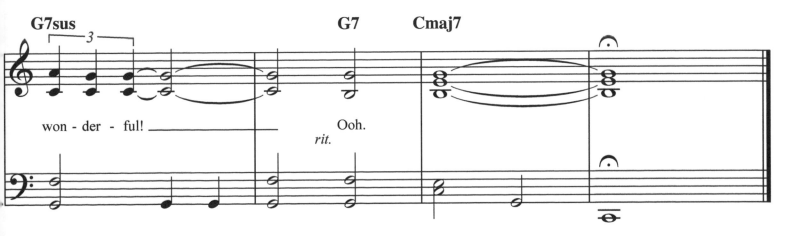

TAKE GOOD CARE OF MY BABY

Words and Music by GERRY GOFFIN
and CAROLE KING

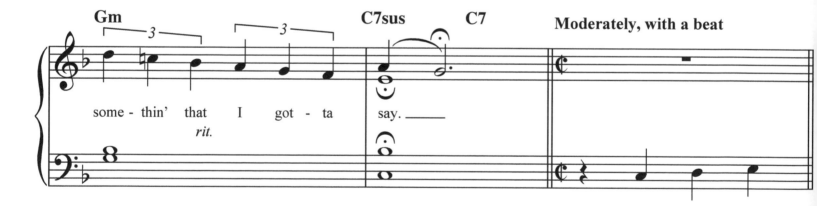

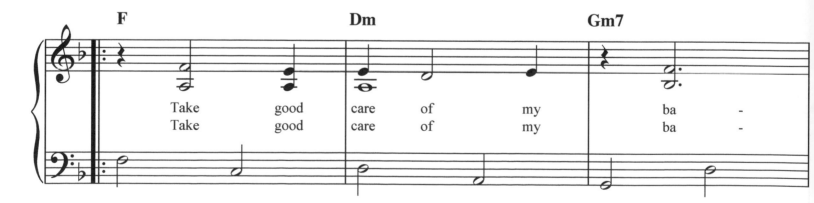

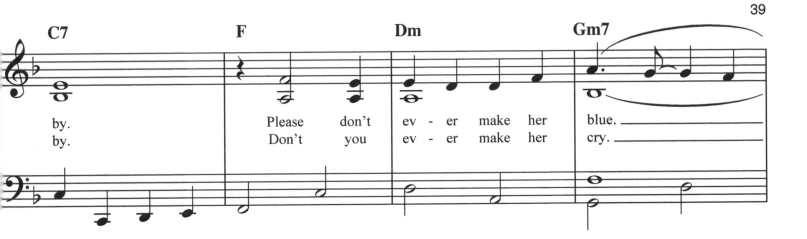

by.
by.

Please don't ev - er make her blue. _____
Don't you ev - er make her cry. _____

Just tell her that you love her, make sure you're
Just let your love sur - round her, paint a rain - bow

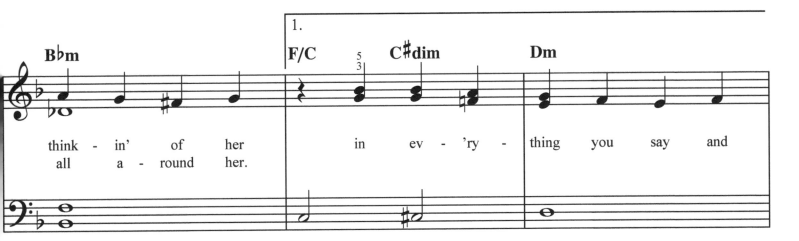

1.

think - in' of her in ev - 'ry - thing you say and
all a - round her.

2.

do. _____ Don't let her see a cloud - y

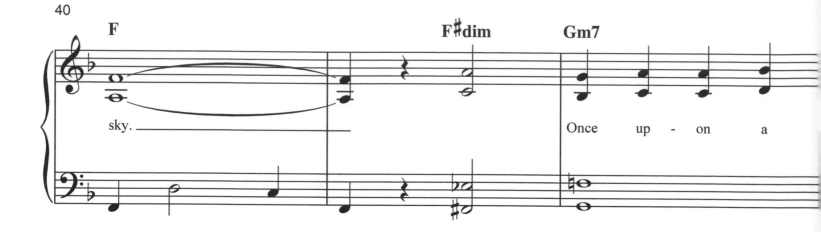

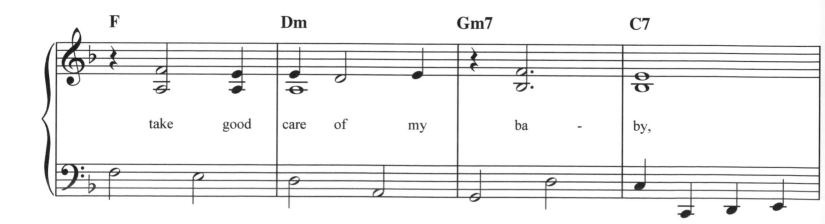

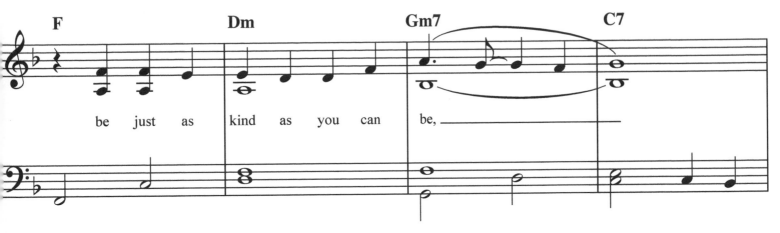

be just as | kind as you can | be, _____

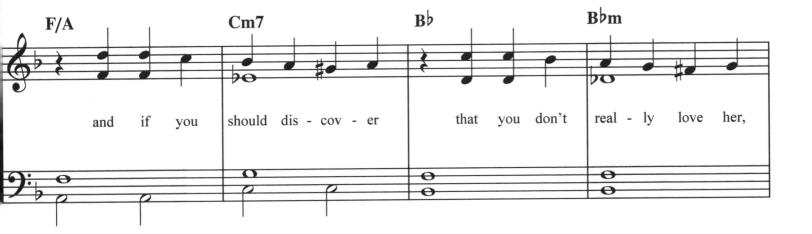

and if you | should dis - cov - er | that you don't | real - ly love her,

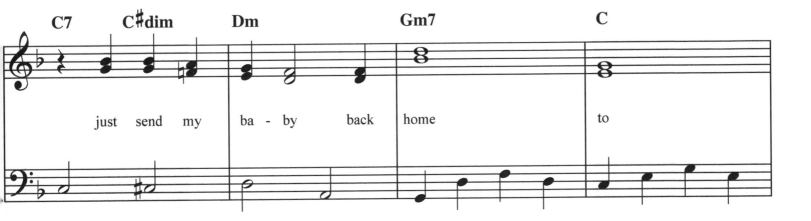

just send my | ba - by back home | to

me. | | Come home to | me.

WILL YOU LOVE ME TOMORROW
(Will You Still Love Me Tomorrow)

Words and Music by GERRY GOFFIN
and CAROLE KING

Moderately, with expression

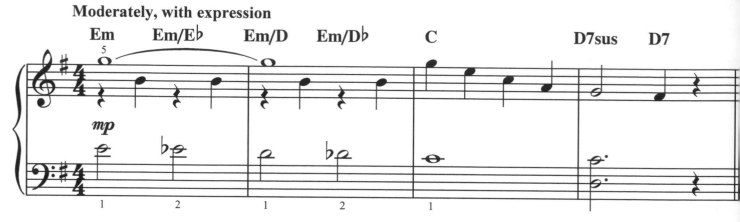

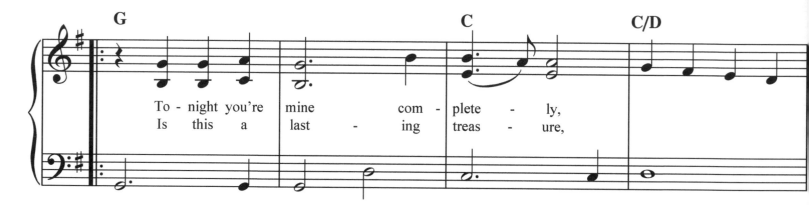

To - night you're mine com - plete - ly,
Is this a last - ing treas - ure,

you give your love so sweet - ly.
or just a mo - ment's pleas - ure?

To -
Can

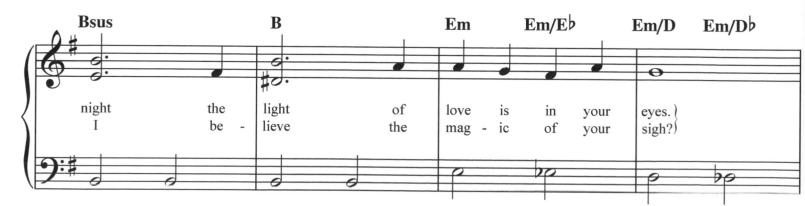

night the light of love is in your eyes.
I be - lieve the mag - ic of your sigh?

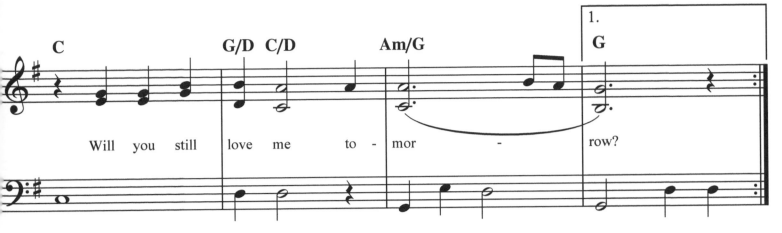

Will you still love me to - mor - row?

row?   To - night   with   words   un -

spo - ken, _____   you   say   that   I'm   the   on - ly

one, _____   but   will   my   heart   be

bro - ken   when the   night ___   meets the

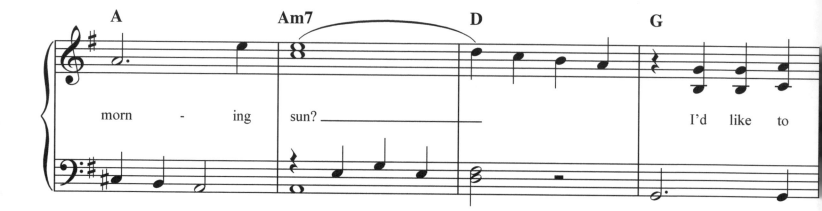

morn - ing   sun? _____   I'd   like   to

know   that   your ___ love   is   love   I

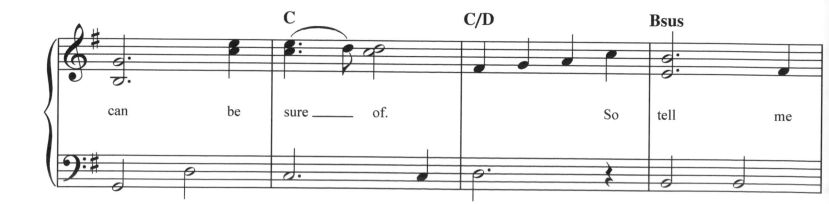

can   be   sure ___ of.   So   tell   me

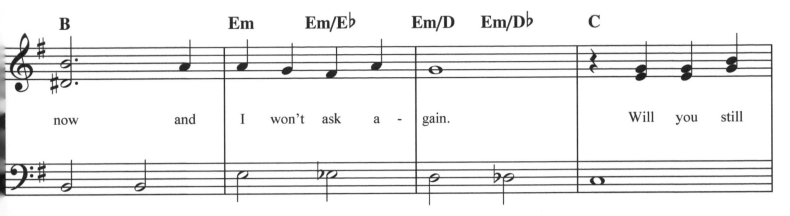

now   and   I   won't   ask   a - gain.   Will   you   still

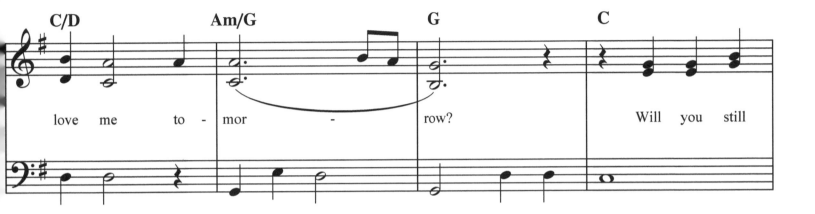

love   me   to - mor   row?   Will   you   still

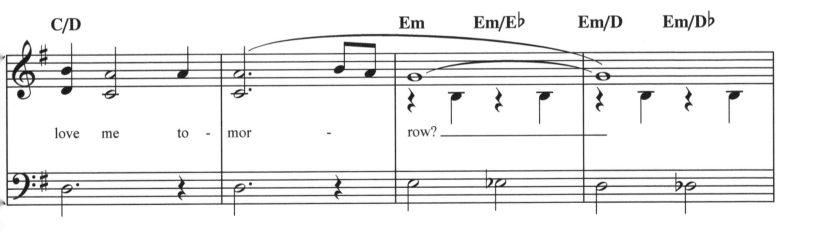

love   me   to - mor   row? _____

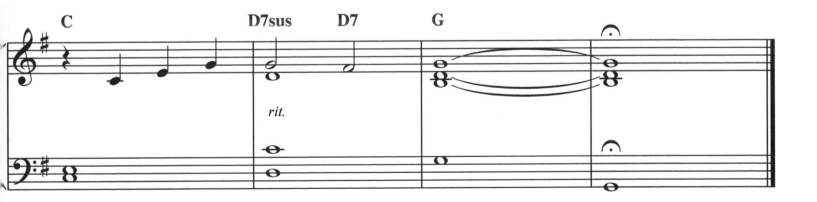

rit.

YOU'VE GOT A FRIEND

Words and Music by
CAROLE KING

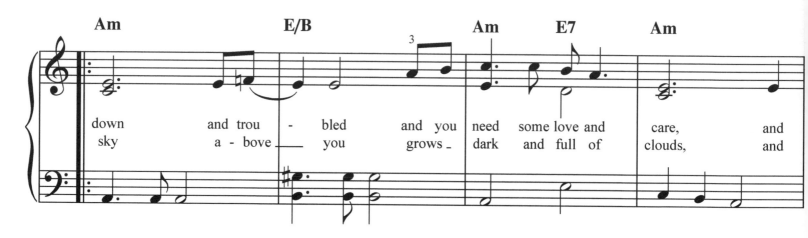

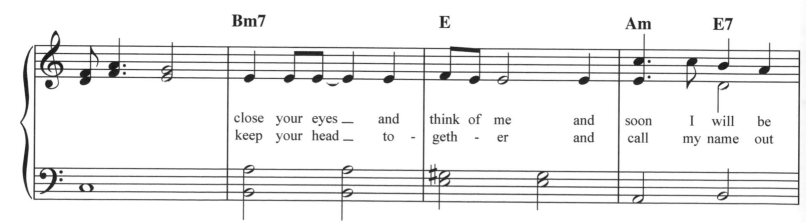

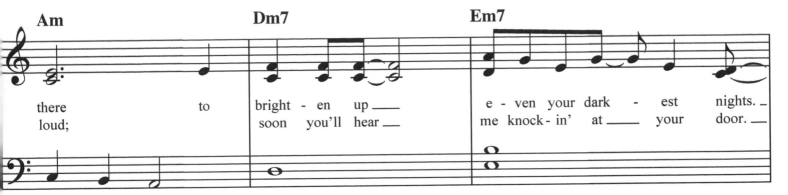

there   to   bright - en up ___   e - ven your dark - est nights. ___
loud;   soon you'll hear ___   me knock - in' at ___ your   door. ___

You just   call   out my name ___   and you

know wher-ev - er I   am   I'll come run - nin'   to see you a - gain. ___

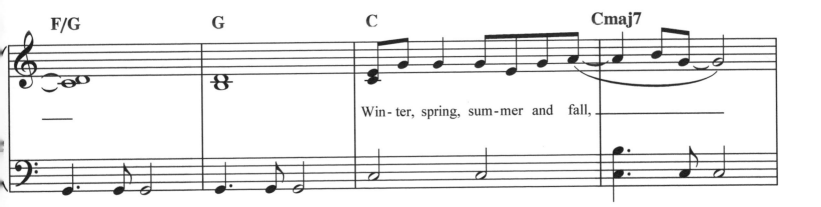

___   Win - ter, spring, sum-mer and fall, ___

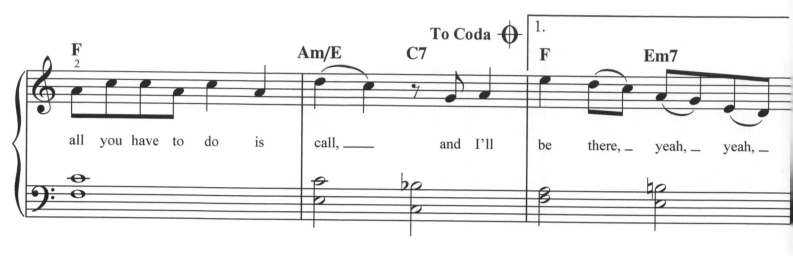

all you have to do is   call, _____   and I'll   be   there, _ yeah, _ yeah, _

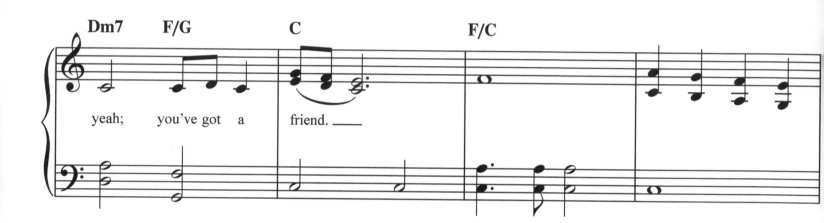

yeah;   you've got   a   friend. _____

If   the   be there, _____ yes,   I   will. _____   Now

ain't it good to know that   you've got   a   friend _ when   peo - ple can be __ so cold? __

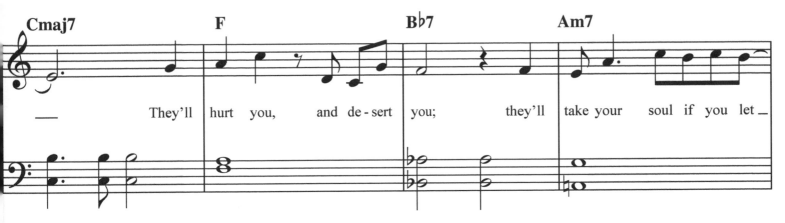

They'll hurt you, and de-sert you; they'll take your soul if you let __

__ them. Oh, but don't you let __ them. You just

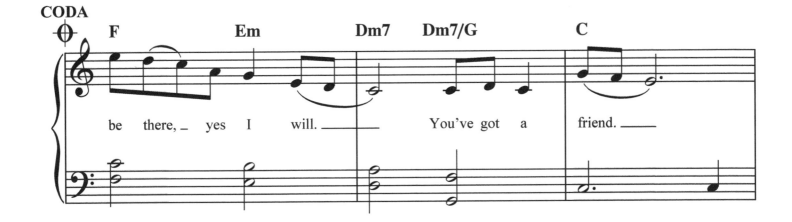

CODA

be there, __ yes I will. __ You've got a friend. __

You've got a friend. __ Ain't it good to know you've got a friend.

YOU'VE LOST THAT LOVIN' FEELIN'

Words and Music by BARRY MANN,
CYNTHIA WEIL and PHIL SPECTOR

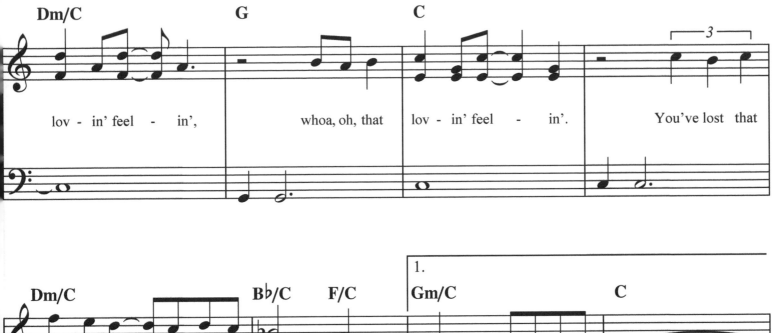

lov - in' feel - in', whoa, oh, that lov - in' feel - in'. You've lost that

lov - in' feel - in'. Now it's gone, gone, gone, whoa, oh. ____

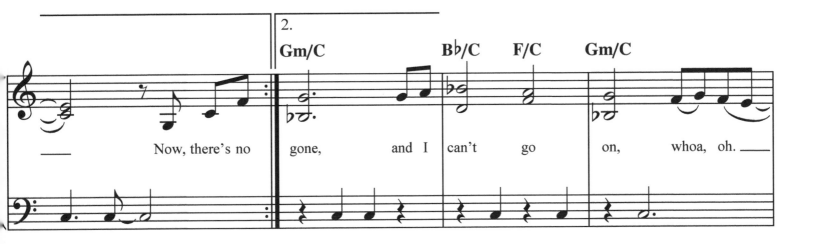

____ Now, there's no gone, and I can't go on, whoa, oh. ____

(You Make Me Feel Like)
A NATURAL WOMAN

Words and Music by GERRY GOFFIN,
CAROLE KING and JERRY WEXLER

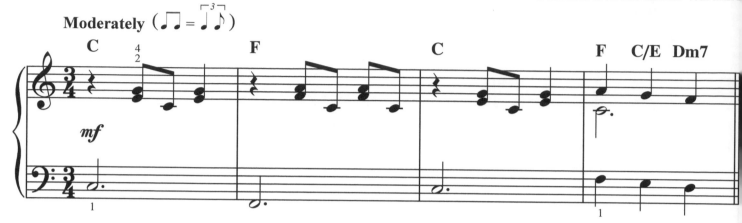

Look - in' out on the morn - ing rain, _____
When my soul was in the lost and found, _____

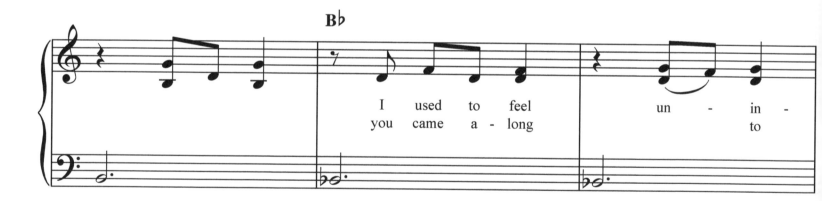

I used to feel un - in - to
you came a - long

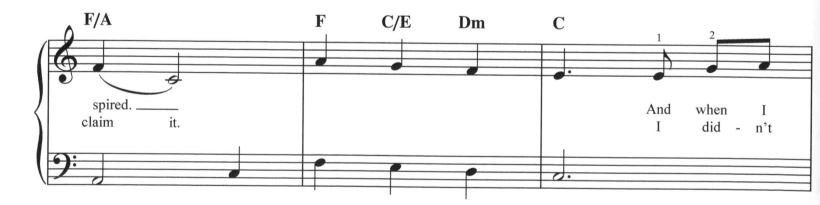

spired. _____ And when I
claim it. I did - n't

knew I'd have to face an - oth - er day, _____
know just what was wrong with me, _____

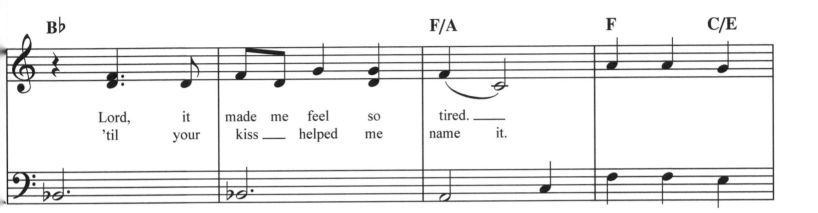

Lord, it made me feel so tired. _____
'til your kiss _____ helped me name it.

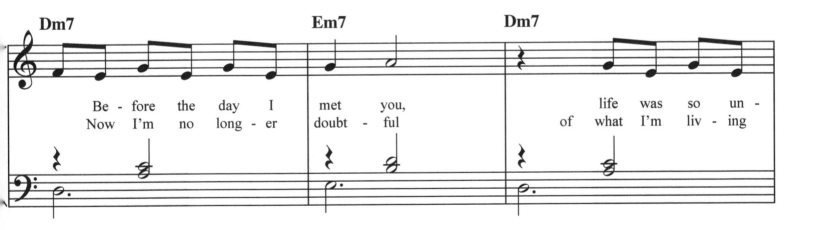

Be - fore the day I met you, life was so un -
Now I'm no long - er doubt - ful of what I'm liv - ing

kind. 'cause Your love was the key to my _____ peace of
for, if I make you hap - py I don't need to do _____

mind, _____ } 'cause you make me ___ feel, _____ you make me ___
more, _____

feel, _____ you make me ___ feel like a ___ nat - u - ral

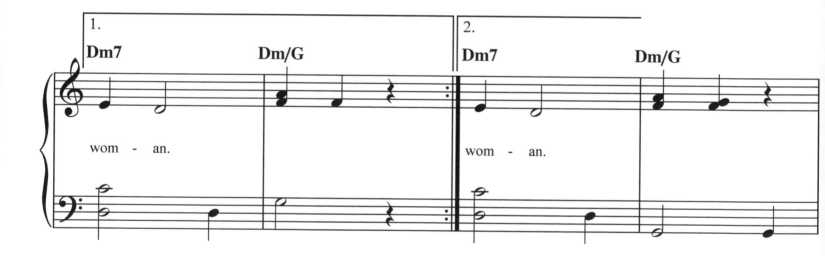

1.
wom - an.

2.
wom - an.

Oh, ___ ba - by, what you've done to me! ___ (What you've

done to me!) _____

F/C **C**

You ___ make me feel ___ so ___ good

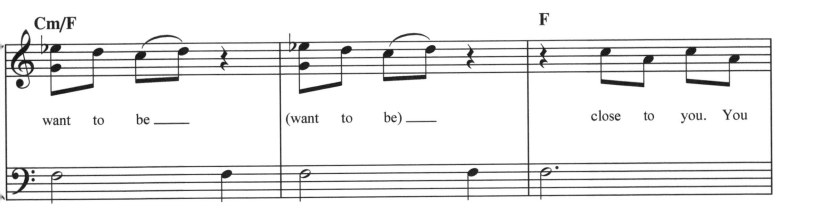

B♭/C

in - side.

(Good in - side.) _

Fmaj7

And I just ___

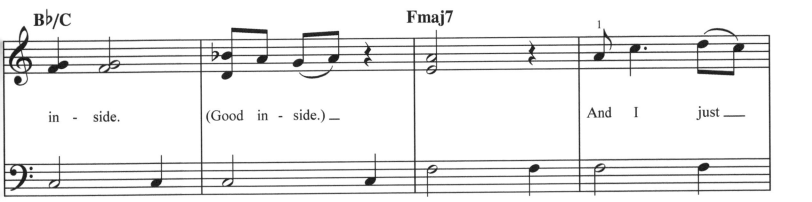

Cm/F

want to be _____

(want to be) _____

F

close to you. You

C/E

make me feel _____ so a - live! _____

Dm7

Dm7/G

You make me

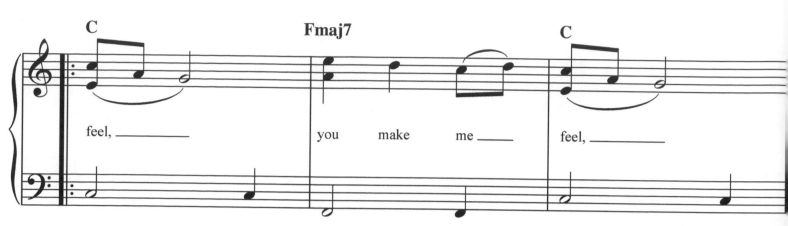

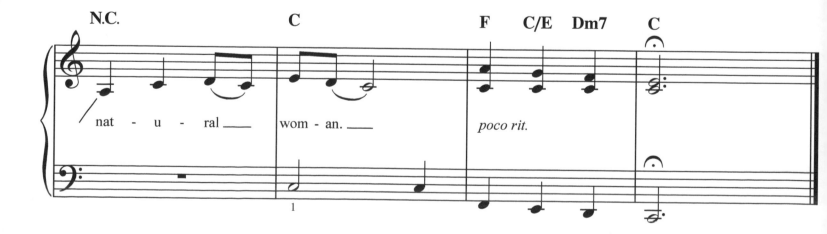